W9-ATN-930

WITHDRAWN

JR. GRAPHIC AMERICAN LEGENDS

JOHNNY APPLESEED

Andrea P. Smith

PowerKiDS
press

New York

Published in 2012 by The Rosen Publishing Group, Inc.
29 East 21st Street, New York, NY 10010

First Edition

Editor: Joanne Randolph
Book Design: Planman Technologies
Illustrations: Planman Technologies

Library of Congress Cataloging-in-Publication Data

Smith, Andrea P.
Johnny Appleseed / by Andrea P. Smith. — 1st ed.
    p. cm. — (Jr. graphic American legends)
Includes index.
ISBN 978-1-4488-5193-5 (library binding) — ISBN 978-1-4488-5224-6 (pbk.) —
ISBN 978-1-4488-5225-3 (6-pack)
1. Appleseed, Johnny, 1774–1845—Juvenile literature. 2. Apple growers—United
States—Biography—Juvenile literature. 3. Frontier and pioneer life—Middle
West—Juvenile literature. I. Title. II. Series.
SB63.C46S64 2012
634'.11092—dc22

[B]

2011001713

J-GN
J-B
APPLESEED
410-7622

Manufactured in the United States of America

CPSIA Compliance Information: Batch #PLS1102PK: For Further Information contact Rosen Publishing, New York,
New York at 1-800-237-9932

Contents

Main Characters

John Chapman (a.k.a. Johnny Appleseed) (1774–1845)
A businessman who sold apple trees. He became known as Johnny Appleseed. He gained fame for planting apple trees throughout Pennsylvania, Ohio, and Indiana. He sold them to settlers.

Fun Facts

- People have been eating apples for over 2 million years.
- The Greeks and the Romans grew different kinds of apples.
- Colonists from England brought apple seeds, or pips, with them and planted the pips in New England.
- Apple cider was a common drink in colonial America.
- Americans eat more apples than any other fruit.
- Nearly 260 million bushels of apples are grown in the United States each year.
- Washington, Michigan, and New York are the largest apple-growing states.

JOHNNY APPLESEED

5

SOON CHAPMAN HAD APPLE **NURSERIES** ALL THROUGH PRESENT-DAY PENNSYLVANIA, OHIO, AND INDIANA.

SHOO, DEER! GET AWAY FROM MY TREES.

HE TRAVELED ALL OVER FROM NURSERY TO NURSERY.

HE **HARVESTED** SEEDLINGS AND **REPAIRED** FENCES.

CHAPMAN HAD A DEEP LOVE FOR ANIMALS.

POOR MOSQUITO!

ONCE, IT WAS SAID, CHAPMAN PUT OUT HIS CAMPFIRE SO THE MOSQUITOES WOULDN'T GET BURNED.

LOOK! THERE'S A RATTLESNAKE!

THERE'S NO NEED TO HURT IT. LET'S JUST SCARE HIM AWAY.

SHOO!

GO AWAY, SNAKE.

16

Timeline

September 26, 1774	John Chapman is born in Leominster, Massachusetts.
1780	John Chapman's father returns home after serving several years under George Washington during the American Revolution.
1797	Chapman sets out for the western frontier.
Early 1800s	Chapman travels to the Northwest Territory where he begins his apple business.
c. 1809	Chapman has thriving apple nursery in Pennsylvania.
1809	Chapman buys land for the first time in Mount Vernon, Ohio.
1812	Chapman works as a scout and warns Ohio settlers of possible Indian attacks.
c. 1828	Chapman has gone west, as far as Fort Wayne, Indiana.
c. 1845	Chapman's orchards covered over 1,200 acres (486 hectares).
March 18, 1845	John Chapman dies in Fort Wayne, Indiana.
1966	The Post Office issues a Johnny Appleseed stamp.

Glossary

appreciate (uh-PREE-shee-ayt) To be thankful for something or someone.

Bible (BY-bul) A work that defines the religious beliefs and rules for people who believe in the teachings of Jesus Christ.

cider mills (SY-der MILZ) Buildings where cider is made.

famous (FAYM-us) Being very well known.

harvested (HAR-vist-ed) Gathered a season's crop.

nurseries (NURS-rees) Places where plants and trees are raised and sold.

orchard (OR-cherd) An area where fruit trees, nut trees, or sugar maples are grown.

pneumonia (noo-MOH-nya) An illness that people can get in their lungs.

repaired (rih-PERD) Fixed something that was broken.

seedlings (SEED-lingz) Young plants or trees grown from seeds.

settlers (SET-lerz) People who move to a new land to live.

tough (TUF) Strong or firm.

unclaimed (un-KLAYMD) Something that does not belong to anyone.

Index

Web Sites

Due to the changing nature of Internet links, Power Kids Press has developed an online list of Web sites related to the subject of this book. This site is updated regularly. Please use this link to access the list:

www.powerkidslinks.com/JGAM/apple